# THE
# LOAN OFFICER
# Revolution

Leading the charge for creating
## REALTOR PARTNERSHIPS
. . . *that actually work*

# RICK ELMENDORF

Printed in the United States of America
Elmendorf, Rick
THE LOAN OFFICER REVOLUTION
ISBN: 978-1-946208-51-4

**Disclaimer**

*This book is designed to provide information for Loan Officers, mortgage experts, and any other person in the real estate industry relative to the content within. It is sold with the understanding that the publisher and author are not engaged in rendering legal, accounting or other professional services. If legal or other expert assistance is required, the services of a specialist should be sought.*

*Because of rapid changes in the industry, this book contains information on the creation and care of professional relationships in the real estate and mortgage lending industry as of press time. Therefore, this text should be used only as a general guide and not as the ultimate source of information for this subject.*

*The purpose of this manual is to educate and inspire. The author and Vervante, Inc. shall have neither liability nor responsibility to any person or entity with respect to any loss or damage caused, or alleged to have been caused, directly or indirectly, by the information contained in this book.*

# DEDICATION

First and foremost, I owe everything I have ever accomplished in business to my God, my Lord and Savior Jesus Christ. On March 16, 1994, I bowed my head in the dimly lit parking lot of Fairfax Baptist Temple on a Wednesday night after service and called on Him to save me (Romans 10:13). It was the best day of my life and what has changed my life and business forever.

To my wife and business partner, Marie. You have been there through thick and thin and have supported my ideas with fervor. You are my confidant and my rock.

Special thanks to my wonderful team. None of this would be possible without the countless hours and excellence in business you display every day. Thank you.

To the fine team at NexGen HBM (Home Buyers Marketing) who have not only prayed for me, but designed an amazing product that has been the basis for so many of my Realtor relationships that exist today.

To Casey Cunningham, CEO of Xinnix Mortgage Academy, who many years ago, helped me understand my team and their roles to support me and gave me priceless insight on building a business around my past clients and database. Thank you.

Finally, a big Thank You to Tim Braheem, my coach and friend. Your leadership has helped me pave the path to many of my recent accomplishments. Your Leadership 360 program is amazing and something all Loan Officers should experience.

*"I'm so proud of the work that Rick Elmendorf has done in writing this much needed book for Loan Originators and Realtors. Rick brings not only an abundance of top producer experience to the pages of this read, but more importantly the heart of a servant. His passion for helping and doing business in an ethical and giving way is exactly why he is such a huge success. I'm honored to call him a friend and a client."*

—Tim Braheem

*"The Loan Officer Revolution is amazing and once I started reading, it was hard to put down. The guidance contained in this book has tactical information that would allow the reader to implement new practices into their business that would lead to explosive results. If you're looking for a path to success as a new loan officer or taking your business to the next level as a seasoned veteran or top producer, I would highly recommend this book."*

—JOHN BIANCHI
Caliber Home Loans - Evp, National Retail Lending

# TABLE OF CONTENTS

# YOUR INVITATION TO MY
## *Revolution*

Being a Loan Officer can be, quite frankly, a thankless job. In fact, I would argue that the whole relationship between the Loan Officer and Realtor is broken. We partner with Agents with the idea of helping each other grow. We work tirelessly to serve our partners and their clients, even so far as helping to procure and convert new clients. Then we find ourselves left at the altar, so to speak, for a competitor who decides to pay for their "marketing," advertise on their website, or pay to stick a sign in the yard. Don't get me started on this rather unsavory side of our business! I've seen this and have experienced it firsthand.

The Loan Officer / Realtor relationships of the past are not working anymore. It's time for change. It's time for a revolution.

That's why I've written this book. In these pages I've shared my strategies for building a successful business as a Loan Officer on the foundation of creating and adding value to the RIGHT kind of Loan Officer / Realtor relationships.

I certainly don't pretend to know everything. I've made my mistakes, learned from them, and made even more. Who hasn't? But what I do bring to the table are more than 20 years of significant volume and doing a lot of things right. Sales tactics to increase loan originations, team building, systems and building long-lasting, value-driven relationships with top Realtors and financial planners—these are all securely in my wheelhouse.

Since 2000 I've been a top-producing Loan Officer and that has been built on the relationships I've created. Last year in 2016, I funded exactly 556 loans for $211,575,354 in volume. (Yes, my company redacted the $1.5 million or so in HELOCS. I say they count!). Of that volume, 258 units (minus HELOCs) for $98.9 million was purchase.

The most outstanding statistic of that year, however, was the 65 Realtors who referred a closed transaction to me in 2016. Proof that this book's subject matter is real, does work, and can transform your business just like it did mine.

I hope you find this book not only really good for your business, but also a blessing and encouragement. Let's get started.

## The question that started it all

### "Rick, how do we get these Agents to work with us?"

It was a balmy 84 degrees in Hawaii and I was on the porch of our room staring out at the beautiful ocean when the email came in. It was Troy and we had been discussing a system to get this group of Agents to work with us. Troy had been encouraging me to start writing down my business tactics on paper and teaching these things that just came naturally to me. I had been asked this question time and time again. What was my system to connect with and motivate Agents to start working with my team? As I sat there staring at my email, I quickly typed the following.

> Troy,
> So, let's just do this. Set up an initial call/meeting to see what we can do for them. If the call goes well, schedule a follow-up meeting or call to implement one of our initiatives in their business plan. Add to our business boost for the consistent follow up. If we choose to partner together, schedule out calls/meetings once a quarter for a year.

This wasn't enough. I knew there was so much more there and the idea for a book was born. For more than 25 years, as I've built a business and created a life I am happy and proud to be a part of, I've always felt a desire to help others along the way. One of my core values is to give without expectation, so I shared my ideas and experiences through everything from emails, to lunches and workshops, and even from the stage at large industry gatherings.

But I realized that answering these questions with just a few thoughts or random tips was only the first step, and there was so much more that I could share. Everyone is different, there is no one-size-fits-all solution, but I knew that the system I'd created and used for my own business would work for anyone in the industry—from Loan Officers to Realtors. I'd been coaching using this system, and watched very different people thrive by applying their own creativity, style and way of doing business to the lessons I shared with them.

I'm not ashamed to share that I'm a Star Wars geek, so often I like to think of the way we choose our Agent partners like the way a Jedi Knight would choose a Padawan learner. The Jedi trains the Padawan in the ways of the force and they become a unit. They protect each other, fight for each other and depend on each other. I really think that this is a perfect depiction of what Loan Officer / Realtor relationships could be. And, honestly, don't we all want to be Jedi's in some way?

What you read here in this book is the structure behind all the advice I found myself giving again and again over the years. Think of it as the foundation of a home, with rooms and a blueprint you can follow to get started. It's up to you to decorate and give your home a story to make your business special and unique and exactly what you want it to be.

I encourage the reader to have a mindset of giving without expectation as we embark on this journey of choosing and even possibly training a real estate Agent. There will be times where hours of hard work go by the wayside. Revolution isn't easy, after all! Remember that the work you do with someone also helps YOU get better. Stay true to what makes you unique, and commit to the things you'll learn here in building up your business. And don't forget the fun! Enjoy what you do. It'll show. And that's truly one of the best secrets for creating a business you really love.

"Always pass on what you have learned."

−Yoda

# Chapter 1

## THE ALMOST
# BIG MISTAKE

---

I almost really messed up. Back in the year 2000, I was working for a company called North American Mortgage and even though I'd been in the business for 6 years, I still really had no clue what I was doing. I hadn't learned to replicate myself, or rather, I hadn't taken the risk to replicate myself. I felt it would be bad for business for me to stop producing to focus on a system of operations. I just didn't have the time, which meant that my business was very "fly by the seat of my pants" and I was constantly reacting.

I did realize that I needed help. So, the first thing did was hire someone to assist me for all loans "in process." This would allow me to focus on originating and not get consumed with the "mind taxing" issues of loans in process. An underwriting condition would never ruin my day again! A good friend of mine whom I had hired for this position saw the need. He suggested we focus on putting in place a core system from Originations to Closing. He said we needed to do this before we did anything else production oriented. I disagreed whole heartedly and got all puffed up and figured he just didn't understand the business. I was busy, I needed to focus on business coming in the door and how to add more relationships, get more leads, get more yeses, learn more sales tactics, etc. That was my focus. Bottom line, I felt like I didn't have time to do any non-dollar producing work.

It's funny how God puts things in your life both good and bad to conform you to where He wants you to be. Let's just say there were a series of events in my life and business that made it very clear that I needed a true system...and fast! What I finally realized was that until I knew where I was going, until I wrote the road map, I would always be reacting. I almost missed it as I was so pig-headed with my focus on what would benefit me now versus seeing the bigger picture. I had to prepare for the business before it was there. It was that year I came up with my 4 Pillars of Business: Business Development, Originations, File Management and Client for Life. I've had the same general system since 2000 and have built on it and refined it over the years with the help of some amazing friends and coaches. This is exactly what I use to help both Loan Officers and Agents with their business.

My point is this, create a system that fits YOU, not others. A system that not only helps others but a system they feel compelled to conform to and not the other way around. (This is especially true for the Realtors you choose to partner with). A very wise man once said, "There are enough people that will do business the way you want to, leave the rest."

# Chapter 2

## SYSTEM
# ENGINEERING

---

As a Loan Officer, you definitely should have a system for what happens with every client from A to Z that includes clear expectations, policies and procedures. Funny enough is that many of us have a semblance of a system, but it's more "second nature" than a tangible system. This is why many loan officers have difficulty building a team and doing more business. All the knowledge is in the brain of the LO and not written down for other to follow (or be taught).

## Ask yourself this:

**Do you have a written- down, consistent way of doing what you do? And do you and your team follow this system every time without exception?**

A great exercise I did years ago was write a Descriptive Account of what going through my process looked like from the eyes of the borrower. (See my Descriptive Account in the resources section). I left absolutely nothing out. I followed the "life of a loan" with the most perfect borrowers having the most perfect process. I started at the very beginning, from how the lead was referred to me, every phone call, every action, when they spoke to me, when they didn't, what my team said, etc. Yes... everything. Wrote it all out. This is how I wanted things to happen and it became the roadmap for the system I have today.

So now I come to the topic of Realtors. Specifically, what is the system I follow for how I choose someone to work with and how I provide value to them. People ask me all the time, "Rick, how do you attract and get these Agents to work with you? And how do you keep them engaged?" I always had answers, and could pitch them in dramatic fashion, but there remained the issue that I really didn't have anything in writing. I didn't have a system. To grow this vertical of my business, I knew that I needed everyone on the same page and so I applied myself to the task of laying out my system for not only how I choose, but also how I execute a plan with every Agent I come across. Let's jump right in.

## Here is a simple break-down of the steps in my system.

1. Evaluate the potential relationship by reviewing any recent experiences along with a quick call or email exchange.

2. Properly engage the Agent and set up an initial call/meeting.

3. Conduct the initial call/meeting. Overview of "The Problem."

4. Schedule and conduct the implementation call/meeting (if needed).

5. Add Agent to your mail and email campaign for consistent follow up.

6. Schedule 6-week coaching if applicable.

7. Schedule out a call/meeting each quarter with re-evaluation at one year mark.

Throughout the rest of this book, we'll dive deeper into each step and I'll share with you how you can apply these steps, along with my insight and experiences, to put you on the path to implementing your own system.

As you progress through the book, I would suggest following the process I share to a "T" and don't skip any steps. I have "been there and bought the t-shirt" for several bad relationships and time wasters in my career and I've used what I learned from those experiences in my system to make sure they don't happen again. Lord willing, following my system will help you attract and engage the right partner, and keep them for life.

*You'll note my referring to "The Problem" throughout this book, a persistent issue in our industry which shows the major dysfunctions of the Realtor's business and the Realtor / Loan Officer relationship. Please see the Resources section for a visual representation provided by NexGen HBM.*

# Chapter 3

## THE AGENT
## BAROMETER

---

I learned a long time ago that there are relationships we should seek out—and ones we should avoid. Learn early to identify and steer clear of the people who bring so much stress and negativity to the relationship that it outweighs any financial benefit.

When it comes to creating connections and forming new professional relationships, I always start out with these general guidelines: *(p.s. these go both ways!)*

1.  Avoid exhausting relationships.

2.  Avoid Agents who like to play "Loan Officer." *(And Loan Officers, don't play Realtor!)*

3.  Seek excellence, regardless of experience.

4.  Seek partners that care about your business.

5.  Seek those that say, "Thank You" and respect your time.

I've been doing this a long time and I've learned that when you're seeking the best kind of relationships, it's important to seek out people who truly want to partner with you. People who are willing to put in the time, energy and work to benefit you both. In fact, I think it's just as helpful to know what you DON'T want as much as what you do. Or, as a very wise Jedi once said: "These aren't the *partners* you're looking for!"

For instance, as you can see from what I've been sharing in this book, it takes time and focus to create positive, lucrative relationships with Realtors and other industry professionals. If you meet someone who balks at having to put in some work to make things happen, or clearly doesn't value your time (very demanding with nonstop questions about loans and business, but not pertaining to a specific transaction), this should put up a red flag as someone you DON'T want to work with.

Trust and respect are two foundational parts of a good professional relationship. Be careful if you run into people seeking to work with you who are known for trying to do your job as well as theirs in order to impress their clients. Each person in a partnership should respect the other's expertise and allow them to do what they do best without interference.

When it comes to other qualities to watch out for—and avoid if you can—they are basically in line with qualities I'd rather not have in anyone I associate with. Foul language, disrespectful, angry or hot-tempered, belligerent, and quick to blame others are a few traits I try to stay away from. And if someone asks you to "pay to play," walk away. End of story.

My goal here is to put a spotlight on the importance of the *right* kind of relationships and how a Loan Officer can help the business of the Realtor, and a Realtor can help a Loan Officer right back. We aren't just the men and women at the bottom of the sales funnel, we are an active part in the sales process...the aide in the conversion of their leads and contacts. A partnership—correction, the *right* partnership—creates more business. And that's good for everyone involved.

In the next chapter, we'll talk about the types of Agents you SHOULD be looking for. But for now, to put what we've discussed so far simply, remember this:

- Set your boundaries and stick to them

- Leave the relationships that don't make you happy.

- Stick to the ones that provide leverage to your business. *(And you to theirs!)*

# Chapter 4

## CHOOSING
## WISELY

---

Sometimes it's hard to tell prior to an initial meeting how a relationship might work out. For this reason, I created a very simple method for choosing the right Agents to work with.

1. Review any recent experience you've had with that Agent. Check with your team and processors and ask for their opinion. You are looking for Agents that you and your team liked and treated your people well during the transaction.

2. Call all parties of the transaction, including the buyer, and ask how it was to work with your "prospective Agent." Side note, making it a point to contact all sides of the transaction is a good habit to get into after the successful closing of a home purchase. What you are looking for is whether these people would recommend that you continue to work with this Agent

3. Thoroughly research them via social media. It's amazing what you'll find, from current Loan Officer relationships to organizations they care about, etc. Based on what you know (or find out) about that Agent, ask yourself if this person provides leverage to my business. This goes beyond just the deals they send.

4. Can you help them? Widely overlooked is not what they can do for you but what you can do for them! If you feel you bring something to the table especially for this Agent, then this should factor in.

The information you're gathering comes down to this bottom line: It's important to use this time to identify certain things about each person to see if you will start or continue to work with them. Ask questions that help you get to the core issues of: Do you have similar core values? Do you like them, would you enjoy working with them well into the future? Will they provide "leverage" to your business?

Remember, this isn't just about choosing new Agents, it's about looking at current ones, reviewing your experiences, seeing how others feel about them, and determining if these are relationships that are good to continue and offer win-win situations for all sides. Once you have completed your research for each potential relationship, decide whether to move on to the next part of the process or let this one go. *Special Note: If you have deemed a contact not to be a good fit, make a CLEAR note of your decision and the reason for your decision in your CRM.*

Personally, the best type of agents I like to work with are **Low-Maintenance / High-Profit.** In fact, even **Low / Low** will work just fine. As I mentioned in my introduction, I couldn't believe my eyes when I ran the report for how many "unique" Agents referred business to us last year. In total, 65 different Realtors referred business to us in 2016. That's a lot of relationships! The secret is that you don't have to manage them all. The solution is having a low maintenance partner that does their job well and leaves you to do yours.

# Chapter 5

## ENGAGE
## PROPERLY

---

This may sound overly dramatic, but the way in which you prepare the initial call or meeting will make or break the rest of the process. Never attempt to jump right into a pitch on this call or email exchange. Invest several minutes connecting and building rapport. This is an important piece to see the engagement level.

Once you have rapport, here is a sample script to help you set up the call/meeting: "(I or Team Lead) would like to connect with you next week about how we can help your business." Then say one or all the following in conversation format.

- We've been successful in really accelerating the business of the Agents we work with.

- Simply put, we have a strategic plan to help our Agents do more and be more efficient.

- The existing relationship between Realtor and Loan Officer is broken and I want to show how we've fixed it to enhance both our businesses.

p.s. I know these scripts may sound corny, but just say them. It's simple and to the point. The key to scripting is to grab the buzz words and just speak naturally.

Then ask, "Can you give me a couple of days you're available next week so I can put it on our calendar?" or "Looks like I have Tuesday and Wednesday open next week for lunch... do either one work for you?" *Note that I am on purpose not trying to nail them with an "alternate of choice close" using language like "which day works best?" sort of thing. People see right through it and I've found it's better to be sincere than try and close in this situation.*

# *Chapter 6*

## THE
# INITIAL MEETING

---

Your very first meeting should be lunch or a 30-minute call maximum. I use this time for getting to know each other and briefly giving an overview of "The Problem" and my solution. Always try to get an in-person meeting, lunch is preferable, but a call will do if necessary or if locations just don't work out. Going out to meet someone for the first meeting is a good thing, so don't shy away from driving a bit of distance to take a new Realtor to lunch!

In this meeting, I focus on accomplishing the following:

1. **Get to know them.** Find out where they are from, their family, how they got into Real Estate, etc. Get to know their "why." Ask them "What was behind your decision to get into Real Estate?"

2. **Let them get to know you.** Briefly share with them your back-ground and how you became a Loan Officer. Show your

passion for the business and your desire to change the current broken Loan Officer / Realtor relationship.

3. **Tell them why you are here.** You are looking for good partners to work with. Tell them that you believe in providing leverage to a partner's business.

4. **Introduce "The Problem"**—the issues that plague the business of a Realtor and stops them from being truly profitable.

    a. The Realtor invests their time and money to generate contacts.

    b. NAR statistic shows that the average Realtor generates 25 contacts per month that are interested in real estate and then only 2 are considered as potential buyers. The other 23 are put in some sort of drip program or ignored all together.

        i. 50% of those 23 contacts will buy something in the next 12 months with 48% of them having a home to sell. The Realtor in the vast majority of these cases are not around when the buyers are finally ready to buy.

        ii. The average patience level of a Realtor is 2-4 weeks to be that source of information to a buyer or seller; however, the buyer timeline is 6-9 months!

    c. Of the 2 buyers converted, there exists no "predictive analysis" system nor substantial and continuous 3rd party endorsement for the Agent. End of story is that many of them move on since the Realtor is also constantly moving on to the new "now" business.

    d.   The Loan Officer played no part in assisting the Realtor in converting those buyers.

**Problem #1**—The Realtor truly focuses on only 2 out of every 25 contacts.

**Problem #2**—The Loan Officer sits passively at the bottom of the sales funnel waiting for the Realtor to do all the work.

5. **Tell them about one or two of your initiatives that solve this problem.** One of the main things I focus on is our ability to manage a large volume of contacts and be a 3rd party endorsement for the Agent. It's important to change the mindset of the Realtor, getting them to realize we, the Loan Officer, should be introduced earlier on in the transaction. We use our initiative to "capture" the buyer and be that 3rd party endorsement. Here are some talking points that seem to resonate well with Agents I speak to:

    a.   The loan officer can better endorse the Realtor than the Realtor can endorse themselves. A very wise man said "Let another man praise you, and not your own mouth, a stranger, and not your own lips."

    b.   The Loan Officer provides important "triggers" to the buying process. Providing simple loan numbers and pre-approval are all tremendous triggers for motivating a client to buy.

    c.   We are a team of trained sales people that work for free with the prime goal of taking the names you provide and turning them into closed transactions for you.

    d.   Clients will often tell us things they won't tell a Realtor. We aren't trying to sell them real estate so they are less guarded with what they say.

    e.    Rick's Favorite: **It's harder to cheat on two than one.**

6. **(Optional) Introduce Home Scout.** If you don't have this at your company, consider getting it. Woven in with the subjects I talk about, above, is offering a service called the Home Scout (offered by NexGen HBM). It is a way for the borrower, Agent and Loan Officer to collaborate within the buyer's personalized (and private) mobile real estate app. It gets the buyer off the existing mobile app they are using (yes they all use one!). It provides a simple business plan for the Agent along with a platform of predictive analysis so you and the agent invest time in only the hot buyers. I've found nothing like it and it's the main tool I use to partner with Agents. It's FREE to the Agent, but not free to the Loan Officer, however just one extra deal a month pays fully for the service. Getting people into "my app" is easy. I will provide more details about this later in the book when I talk about implementation meetings, but I like to hold the carrot of a very simple script I use to capture buyers. "Which app or website are you currently using to get real estate information?" And whatever they say next I say, "May I please give you something better?" (or) "Realtors have the MLS, you don't. Zillow and other public search sites are not direct MLS feeds. I can actually get you my access" (or) "access just like an agent". I send a link or have them download the app. Easy. This is just one way I capture every buyer you send me.

At first glance, everything I've covered here may seem like a lot, but I assure you that with practice you can make "The Problem" a good elevator speech lasting 20 seconds or less, and offer a more detailed review of everything else in under 10 minutes (I call it the 10 Minute Meeting). For in-person meetings, you can expand a lot more. And for a non-lunch, you could even set up a brief slide presentation.

As an example, check out a presentation that I've used in the past: **http://presentation.loanwithrick.com**

# Chapter 7

## THE
# INITIAL MEETING

---

At the implementation meeting you will specifically show your contacts how you will implement your initiatives to help their business. (Use a service like Join.me if not local). Be specific and have one or two things you focus on that you can put into action right away. Track and measure this.

Here are examples of things I have implemented with my Agents.

1. **Get the EMA.** This is my mortgage analyzer which gives the client a purchase worksheet to perfectly calculate all sorts of numbers for their upcoming purchase. *Note: Most of us have some kind of spreadsheet that do mortgage numbers... give it a name! Knowing their numbers is the biggest trigger to buying a home. It's something an Agent can easily sell when speaking to every contact! Here is the script: "Have you heard

of the mortgage analyzer? There is a great Loan Officer in my area that has this amazing spreadsheet he gives out to people buying a home. You can use it to calculate perfect numbers for the purchase of a home and even calculate things like how much in seller concessions you would need and even how much cash you would get from the sale of a home. We have a website and are able to track the source on the back end and capture it for our Agents. If you don't have a website for them to request the analyzer online, then have the Realtor "group text" the buyer and you to ask for a copy of your buyer worksheet.

2. **Home Scout.** My tag line is this: "Finally, a private MLS search for the consumer. Search for like a Realtor." It's really a simple sell.

   a. Agent asks this question to every contact. "What site or app are you using to get real estate information?" (Response). Regardless of response, say "May I offer you something better?"

   b. Agent gives instruction to download the app and VIP code. Or they can provide a unique link that will auto-sign the client up. Here is an example of one I've put together. **http://scout.redteamlending.com**

   c. Post content on Facebook to auto-sign up buyers for Agent. Here's an example of a post for an Agent: **http://hbmexample.loanwithrick.com**

3. **The Ultimate Homebuying Experience.** This is something unique to Caliber Home Loans that Agents are using to generate new home buyers. Here is a press release: **http://digitalmortgage.loanwithrick.com**

a. Sell an experience NOT a product. Nobody really cares about "home ready" or the new 100% program or the next great buy down product. They want the experience of buying a home. Dive into the experience. Sell the "after state" i.e. what they will feel after they buy. This could be the payment on their new home and how easy it is to become a home owner.

b. Sell the benefits of owning. Renting versus owning is a huge issue with many clients making the mistake of renting and damaging their financial future in the process. A great tool to show this is MBS Highway's Rent vs Own calculator. You can inquire at **www.MBShighway.com**

4. **Coaching.** This is 6 weeks long and probably the best way to add value to an Agent partner. There are core principles to doing business on the mortgage side that I feel extend very well to the real estate side. I will warn you that if you choose to coach an Agent that you take it easy and commit to no more than 1 or 2 at a time. When I coach an Agent, I take on their success or failure as my own. You will be investing both your time (which is money) into their business, learning to know their business almost as much as they do. It's not easy but the rewards are long lasting. I have had some Agents where I have invested hours of time and watched them build a million-dollar business, yet still end up using other Loan Officers. It's all part of the game. Coaching at its core is giving without expecting anything in return. We'll review this in great depth in Chapter 8.

# *Chapter 8*

## FOLLOW-UP
# CAMPAIGNS

---

This is the easy part, adding Agents to campaigns for consistent follow up. I have several ways for staying top of mind with Realtors:

1. **Email Campaign.** You can use the Happy Grasshopper or another auto-email program like that. If you use Salesforce like me, you can have a dynamic report or group of every Agent you've ever dealt with. That way you can send personalized messages. Your email campaign can contain video as well.

2. **Mail Campaign.** My company has this thing called business boost. For $5/month per Agent they get in the mail a fun trinket and different marketing item at the beginning of the month. This is a bit of a pain to manage seeing that mailing addresses change. Make sure you have someone managing this so you don't end up throwing money out the window to

bad addresses. If your company doesn't do anything like this, it's easy to find a service that does.

3. **Blogging.** If you don't blog, you need to. You should have all your Agents read your blog regularly. Call them and make them subscribe. **www.blogger.com** is a good one and **www.activerain.com** is also a fine service. The idea is a weekly (or even daily) blog about what is going on in the mortgage industry. A good tip is to use the market wrap from MBS Highway or even something your company does at the end of the day and just put your own voice to it. If these Agents are looking to YOU for insight into the mortgage business, then you are top of mind, not the other guy. Your blog can also give a voice to your team as well as provide marketable content for down the road. What I mean is have them write some blog articles! You review it, write a quick intro and post it. Some general tips for content ideas: Something happens? Blog about it. Got a loan through in a crazy way? Blog about it. Get pissed about another Loan Officer missing a simple guideline or you saving a deal? Blog about it. Make them teachable moments. Be unforgettable, be epic, be funny, be encouraging, and be helpful.

4. **Events.** A Loan Officer team on the West Coast has this as their one thing to stay in touch with Agents and procure business. It's called BBM (Business Building Monthly) and it's a monthly event that they showcase a topic or have one of their Agents speak to the group.

5. **Movie Events.** This is the best way in my opinion to partner with an Agent and get in front of their buyers and clients. I like to do these individually where you and the Agent would be in front of all their clients. We just invite their clients, not ours. Buy the movie, no concessions, and it shouldn't cost you more than $800-$1000 to fill up a 150-200 seat theater after you split

it 50/50. (Yes, this is compliant!) Another idea which is more shotgun effect impactful is to host a "Realtor Movie Event." Invite all your Agents and their kids. Note: for all the movies, show the movie on the Saturday morning following release. Show something big like Star Wars or a cool G-rated movie so they bring their kids. You want them to come and bring the kids, not drop off their teenagers at your event! (*had that happen :/)

# Chapter 9

# COACHING
## YOUR AGENT

---

This is a rather large step so be prepared to have your head spin. Coaching is the absolute best way to add value to an Agent partner. I think about my business coach Tim Braheem and just how special he is to me because of his mentorship and friendship. I'd be hard pressed to ever be coached as well by anyone else. Likewise, coaching a Realtor can help lock down the relationship for you. However, remember that as a coach you make yourself vulnerable. You may invest a lot of time and effort to only get nothing out of the relationship. Or it may be that the coaching just didn't stick. Bottom line, having the right heart going into coaching is important. Coaching at its core is giving without expecting anything in return. Accept this, or don't do it. Below is my attempt to outline my style of coaching and provide a framework for how to coach a Realtor.

*Side note: It's a wonderful thing when you invest in the life of another person. You will not only have gain professionally but personally as well. This is regardless of whether or not the relationship lasts.*

## The 6-week coaching system is as follows:

- **Week 1**—The defining statement, the prerequisite, core values/ initiatives and business vitals

- **Week 2**—Business development and the 4 pillars

- **Week 3**—Origination of a contact

- **Week 4**—File management

- **Week 5**—Client for life

- **Week 6**—Review, recap and commitment!

After each step, I give the Agent homework, taking time to review it at the beginning of the next session. I also take copious notes and email the Agent a recap of each coaching session. At the end of your 6 weeks, I suggest writing a full synopsis of your time together and what you both learned. Dress it up and make it something they could never throw away. One way could be to take all the write-ups and make a hard-cover book!

# *Week 1*
# YOUR BUSINESS VITALS

Week 1 is about getting to really know each other and analyzing the Agent's business. Plan on a minimum of 1.5 to 2 hours for this initial meeting, because it's going to be like sweeping up a dirty house! This week is about sharing perhaps the most important aspect to your coaching together, which is, getting absolutely, unequivocally, laser focused on what can and will move your business forward. We will move through what I call the defining statement, prerequisite of business, core values, core initiatives and summary of our business vitals. The cool thing is that I'm helping the Agent come up with these. My feeling is that it's important not to just give homework, but to be an active part in defining the business of your Agent. Share yours first and help them define theirs.

**The Defining Statement.** A defining statement is more than a slogan, it's what you are. It's your core purpose and it summarizes in a succinct way what your business is about. Here's mine:

## My Defining Statement:
### Home financing the way it should be...EASY.

With this statement, I propose to make the process EASY. Most people would say getting a mortgage is hard or just flat painful. We choose to make everything about home financing different and EASY. Your defining statement should permeate your speech, writing and everything you do. For me, it revolves around EASY.

I've helped every Agent I coach come up with their defining statement. It's exhilarating to give another person something that is so core to their business and YOU gave it to them! One Agent had a very difficult time coming up with the defining statement. So, we broke it down. For them it was about Integrity, Quality, Professionalism, and Respect. Just talking about it got the juices flowing and in a brief time we came up with "Setting a New Standard in Real Estate". This just rolls off the tongue now: "Here's what we do for you Mr. Buyer or Seller. Because to us it's all about setting a New Standard in Real Estate." Bottom line, it's why they do what they do. And it's beautiful to see this in action.

**The Prerequisite for all business:** Defining what you say "YES" and "NO" to.

Before going deeper, we must set some ground rules. I had the opportunity to meet and speak briefly with Darren Hardy. If you don't know who he is, Darren is a very accomplished businessman and speaker. He has had the opportunity to interview some amazing and highly successful people thus far in his career. Steve Jobs, Joel Osteen, and Warren Buffett, just to name a few. Now I'm not normally tongue-tied, but I literally stood there stammering like an idiot trying to state my problems. After finally getting my mouth to move, I explained to Darren that I felt like I was on the cusp of doing something great, but having trouble finding that laser focus he spoke about. I mean, how do you find and narrow down to the 1 to 3 things that you double down on to make you great? He told me that everything I do in business should:

1. Align with my core values
2. Be something I enjoy doing
3. Impact and provide leverage for my life and business

If they do, then say YES.

If they don't, say NO.

**Core Values:** Peeling back the layers of what makes you, well, you!

I used to have a ridiculously long list of core values. There were at least 12 of them and most, albeit niceties in business, were just lip service. Treat the client right, respond quickly, blah blah blah. Seriously, who cares? I needed something real to hang my hat on. Since everything we do in business can't pass GO until it aligns with our core values, I need to define what those are. Core Values are the non-negotiables of your business and life. You will help the Agent clearly define what is Core to them. Here are mine as an example:

# My Core Values

## Honor God in life

## Be excellent in business

## Give freely without expectation

## HAVE FUN

Note that these values are the expectation, but I won't kid myself that they are the reality 100% of the time, every day of the week. Have firm values, but don't beat yourself up if you fall a little short.

## Core Initiatives: What is my offer?

Next is to clearly define the core initiatives. These are the things you do that will prove the defining statement and meet all prerequisites of business. It's how you fulfill your core purpose. Ask yourself, what does this Agent do that is special? What do they offer that is cool and unique? You may have a laundry list of things they do, but don't get carried away. The idea is to have focus and what core incentives are going to move the needle in their business. As an example, here are mine:

# My Core Initiatives

## EMA

## Home Scout

## Mortgage Expert Review

## Ultimate Homebuying Experience

**EMortgage Analyzer (EMA):**
Run scenarios, pre-qualify, savings analysis with no surprises!

1. **Purchase Analyzer**—Play Loan Officer! Construct your perfect mortgage and pre-approval letter!

2. **Refinance Analyzer**—Know exactly how a refinance could save you money.

3. **Rent vs Own Analyzer**—Is it smarter to buy or rent?

4. **Crash Course**—Teaching the A, B, C's of mortgage numbers.

**Home Scout:**
Finally, a private MLS search for the consumer. Gain control and search for your dream home like a Realtor. Provides predictive analysis and content marketing for the Realtor as well as looping the Loan Officer in so they can collaborate and work together as a team to convert the buyer. This is POWERFUL. It's harder to cheat on 2 than 1!

**Mortgage Expert Review:**
Ensure you have the right loan structure for your home purchase and existing loans. Have a true professional actively manage your mortgage debt so it always fits within your short- and long-term financial objectives.

1. **Expert Advice**—Loan structure and debt management.

2. **Second Look**—Guarantee a closed transaction and savings for all parties.

3. **Annual Review**—A financial review to ensure the mortgage and existing structure fits within the short and long-term financial objectives.

**Ultimate Homebuying Experience:**
Tired of the hassle in getting a mortgage? Caliber Home Loans' new fully digital mortgage will close loans in 10 days or less. Redefining the Homebuying Experience. **www.ultimate.loanwithrick.com** to view.

**My 3 Vitals:** My simple, laser-focused, goals for my business.

Some call it the ONE thing. Some say Highest or Best Use, or other terms like Laser Focus. Warren Buffett said, "For every 100 great opportunities that are brought to me, I say 'NO' 99 times." He goes on to say, "The difference between the successful and the very successful is that they say no to almost everything." Steve Jobs was asked once what he was most proud of. He replied, "I am proud of all the things we do, but I am most proud of what we don't do." Steve Jobs told Michael Dell, "You make a lot of great stuff, but you also make a lot of crap... stop making the crap!"

My favorite quote is from Bruce Lee, "I am not afraid of the man who practices 10,000 kicks. I fear the man who has practiced one kick 10,000 times."

This is where you can help the Agent get focused on what they do every day. Here are my 3 Vitals that drive everything I do regarding business. These 3 literally run my day and that of my team.

## My 3 Vitals

### Be the #1 Loan Officer for my Database

### Create new purchase business

### Empower my team

Here is an example of what I did for another Agent. It was clear to me what she really wanted to do... or more importantly what she needed to be doing. We boiled it down to five things. Nothing more, nothing less:

1. Meet new buyers and sellers.
2. Show homes.
3. Negotiate contracts.
4. Attend closings.
5. Throw Parties.

This may seem simplistic, but the "ah-hah" moment, the clarity that we arrived at was surreal. Do your 5 things and hire someone to do everything else. Simple. Regardless of what you call these things (vitals, big 3, etc.), to have traction in my business I know that I must avoid DISTRACTIONS. Distractions are the #1 thing that affect productivity. Saying YES to the right things is not as important as saying NO to the wrong ones.

I think you get the gist and moral of the story here. Be laser-focused and dedicate your time to only a few things. Darren Hardy summarizing hundreds of the successful people he has interviewed boiled it down to 3 things.

**DELETE, DELEGATE and DOUBLE-DOWN on your vital(s).** Deleting means to say "NO" to anything that is not one of your vitals. Delegating means getting everything off your plate that isn't your highest and best use. Doubling-Down means going deep in your vitals and keeping a laser focus to the movers of your business.

If something doesn't help me stay true to my vitals, I say NO... no exceptions.

That's laser focus.

# Week 2

# ESTABLISH THE 4 PILLARS OF BUSINESS AND BUSINESS DEVELOPMENT

The 4 pillars of business are: Business Development, Origination of a Contact, File (or process) Management, and Client for Life.

**Business Development** focuses on the activities and systems in place to get people to inquire about your product or service. It's how you get your clients. In this step, I like to focus on one or two key ways to attract business and avoid distractions.

People say that the hardest part of our business is getting the business. While that may be true, to a point, I often have observed that most people make it much harder than it should be. We allow the distractions of life to permeate our day. We become lazy and don't do the things we know we should do to get business. The best advice I give people for getting more business is this: "Be prepared to work really hard for the next 90 days. Only after 90 days will you have enough thrust to really get your business moving." Todd Duncan once told me that a rocket expends 90% of its fuel just to get out of the atmosphere. It's the same with business, so put forth maximum effort early on and expect to go full speed for the first 90 days. Commit to it.

One of the ways I recommend spending some of the 90-day fuel is with good old fashion, belly-to-belly contact and re-connection. Meet, greet, and kiss babies. Plan daily activities where you are prospecting for new business. Reach out to your sphere. If you don't have one, create one. Have Facebook? Contact your friends and ask for help. Message them, call them, text them. Tell people what you want: "I'm refocusing on my Real Estate business and really need your help." Or, "My goal is to become the premier Realtor in (location) and I figured I would start with my friends for help." Something along those lines.

Another way to spend the 90-day fuel is to meet up with people of influence within your spheres or potential 3rd party endorsers. This could be a financial planner (a major source of business) or it could be an accountant or attorney. Maybe it's someone in HR at a company you know, or you have a friend that's a manager somewhere. Make a point to get belly-to-belly to all those people who could be your ambassadors.

Setting up a consistent email marketing campaign is also paramount during the first 90 days. Your first email should be a reconnect letter. Share your goal is and let them know how they can help.

Lastly, develop the mode by which you want people to come into your world. In other words, if you could define the life of a perfect client, how would it start? Would they email you? Would they call? Would they complete a form or just apply online? Define it and create your sales funnel to fit that mode. Write it out and get super clear on how you want your business to come in to you.

# Week 3

# ORIGINATION OF A CONTACT

This is the point where we convert someone from a lead to a contact and opportunity. During Week 3, I review the system of conversion. What you say, how you present your core offerings, etc. the key for success in this step is to BE CONSISTENT.

1. **Map out a system for following-up.** Be clear about each team member's responsibilities. Everyone has a "highest and best use," and one of the things I work on is not only to define that but to ensure that my team knows it and doesn't allow deviation. In my world, my team knows that I am best used for making it rain, talking to clients, and solving problems. Paperwork and getting lost in the minutia of loans in process are not my thing. My team knows this, so they shield me from involvement in the areas that are not my highest and best use.

2. **Next, clearly lay out the steps that will happen for each client.** What is your goal? In my world, as a Loan Officer, it is to get them to submit a loan application, use my initiatives, and say "yes" to us handling their loan.

   For a Realtor, it's different. Perhaps the key is a signed buyer or listing agreement. In that case, you'll map out the steps that need to happen to obtain your specific goals. For example, do you meet them in person? Is there an initial call? Or maybe a set schedule of emails? Here is what I have found to work well for the Agents I coach:

   a. Schedule a face-to-face meeting. This is where you nail it. Belly-to-belly for coffee, lunch or whatever. Personally, I don't like it when buyers are required to "come in" to the office. Everything you need to do can be done at a convenient location for everyone involved. Some people might say never do this at the home and bring them into the office because it puts you in more of a power position. I disagree. Years in sales tells me that if you make the client comfortable first, then they buy. If you don't, and they buy anyway, they'll often get cold feet and change their mind later.

b.  Set clients up with one of your initiatives. This could be home scout, or it could be something of your own design. For example, one Agent I coached would tour prospective homes for his buyers, compiling a top-tier list for them based on their specific needs. This extra leg work really stood out in a client's mind.

c.  Have a consistent follow up campaign. After the initial meeting comes the "black hole" of Real Estate. Most Realtors have about a 2 to 4-week patience level with new clients. The problem is that the average buyer timeline is 6 to 9 months! I suggest a very simple and cheap email service called Happy Grasshopper. It sends automated emails that you set up ahead of time on a schedule, keeping your name in front of your contacts. An even better option is Home Scout from NexGen HBM. This is the service I mentioned earlier and is the only way to have any sort of predictive analysis and forecasting in the Realtor's business. Having your own mobile app for a buyer's home search that is tied directly into you and your lender as a 3rd party endorsement is just fantastic. Oh, and it's free to the Realtor! You can expect 2 to 3% of active buyers to write contracts every month, making it a numbers game for how many people you want to use your app. For example, if you have 100 users on your app, that would equal 3 closings a month. If you're interested, you can find out more at **https://www.nexgenhbm.com/**

3. **Find your YES point.** The goal in this stage is to get the client to say YES, so you need to clearly define what YES means to you. For a Realtor, it could be a signed buyer or listing agreement. Everything in this stage pushes toward the YES point. You are DONE after the YES and it moves to the next stage.

p.s. Defining the "black holes" and developing crucial and constant follow up systems will lead to higher conversion rates and more referrals. Follow up during the home search phase and after pre-approval is the absolute best time to produce new business. It's when the reticular is activated! People are much more likely to refer people when they are in the process!

*Special Note: The Loan Officer should be an active part in the conversion process of the agent's contacts. It's that 3rd party endorsement! If I know my partners "steps" then I can encourage the buyer to take them!*

# *Week 4*

# FILE MANAGEMENT

This is the nitty gritty of what happens to a contact after they say "YES" to working with you. It's perhaps the easiest stage of the process to mess up and therefore the most important. This part must be very high touch and provide consistent content marketing. The client is at their most heightened state to not only refer you, but they are asking themselves constantly, "am I happy doing this right now?" What sometimes happens is that the client may be happy with what they are doing, just not who they are doing it with.

This week, your goal is to focus on creating or refining the process for handling a client after they say YES. A good exercise is to write everything down that the client goes through, from the second they meet you, to closing on their loan or new home. I call this the "Descriptive Account"—(See my example in the resource section)

What you are looking for is that break-point—the YES. Perhaps already defined in last week's exercise, the YES is the start of the handoff. In my opinion, this is where you as a salesperson MUST delegate and let go. All the follow-up emails, content marketing, paperwork, simple phone calls, etc. can be handed by a team member, or even an automated service. Your focus is to proactively touch the client at key points during the process. Injecting yourself in these key points will keep you (personally) top of mind.

What about non-negotiables? In that list (or ultimately your Descriptive Account) you made detailing everything that happens for the client, several items are going to pop out that are non-negotiable. These are things that happen every time, no matter what, and must be measured. Help your Agent define these. For example, I defined 4 things that happen after the YES that can blow up a transaction. Conversely, by knowing these 4 things and dealing with them proactively, my team and I look like heroes.

Oh, and don't forget to let your customers know that you are dealing with these issues, and you will be following up. You'll just keep looking better and better!

## My incoming phone call rule

If a client calls in, I only want them calling for one (or both) of the following reasons.

1. **They have a referral for me,**
   or...
2. **They call to say Thank You!**

Anything other than this means I didn't communicate as well as I should have and perhaps need a system to proactively handle that which they called about.

## The 4 things that can blow up a loan or make you a hero

*Note: These are my non-negotiables. Outlining mine for the Agent really helps define theirs!*

1. **The Loan Approval**
   Obviously if your loan isn't approved, you suck. Just kidding! It means there are going to be countless issues. Making sure you have a doable deal up front OR that you are delivering bad

news early is paramount. On the flip side, you want to give the good news of a loan approval out to the buyer and all Agents. I am shocked that Loan Officers aren't using this opportunity to call borrowers, buyers and listing Agents when the loan is approved. It's the happiest phone call ever! One of the things my company does is send a text message when the loan is approved, and many times the borrowers are so excited that they beat us to the punch and call in! Automation in this case is nice, but don't skirt the tremendous opportunity to make a personal connection with a loan approval notification.

2. **Appraisal Notify**

   Another line in the sand. Nothing happens without a good appraisal, so checking it and sharing the news when it comes in, and the value, makes you look great.

3. **10-day Prior Review**

   There is nothing worse than finding a mistake in the loan amount, loan docs, borrower name spelling, or anything else right before closing. This is a great time to ensure, and let everyone know that things are on track.

4. **Final CD Review**

   These are the final closing documents and we do this at minimum the day before closing. Closing on a loan or new home should be a celebration not a surprise.

5. **Bonus Step: At Closing Visit or After Closing Touch**

   Do one or the other. In my world, I delegate 1 through 4 but I personally handle #5. I make sure to reach out to every contact that was a part of the transaction after closing. I'm the last voice they hear and the last email they receive. If you are doing a closing call, schedule this weekly on your calendar, i.e. run the report of all closed loans each Friday for the previous week.

# Week 5

# CLIENT FOR LIFE

When you think of a client for life, what goes through your head? To me, it's a client who is a raving fan, who not only does every loan with me, but refers to me everyone they know that needs a mortgage. It's my goal to be that #1 Loan Officer (the go-to) to everyone in my database. In designing a Client for Life strategy, I tend to focus on a few very simple things to stay top of mind. It's my job with the Realtor to help create or refine existing activities to consistently procure business from existing clients.

We all know that it's cheaper to market to and get business from a past client that it is to generate a new client. Here are a few things I've done—some free, some paid, all simple—to make that true:

## Annual Reviews

It may seem like I have my act together at this point, but really I'm not even close to where I want to be when it comes to reviews. Right now, our focus has been mostly on proactively reviewing clients we know we can help. We are actively managing their mortgage, which is great don't get me wrong, but we are missing so much by not having more consistent, proactive, annual reviews with EVERY CLIENT. (*Note to self: Get on this!*)

Remember, just because someone may not need to buy, sell, refinance, etc. doesn't mean they don't know someone else who does. Staying top of mind is crucial. Additionally, during the annual review, look to connect your client to 3rd parties who you know would endorse YOU. Maybe your client doesn't have a financial plan, get them a financial planner referral! Maybe they are planning on a renovation project, get them a contractor. Look for ways to deepen the relationship and provide value.

## Watch for "Thank You"

My father who was (and at 90 years old is) a great salesman taught me to really respect the words "thank you." He said that whenever he heard those words, he now was given permission to ask for something. If you hear "thank you" come out of the mouth of your client, it's OK to ask them for help. Good people love to help good people. Don't rob your client of the blessing to help you.

## Cheesy email campaigns

For years, I used a service called "Happy Grasshopper." The emails were literally about nothing but it did bring in business. I currently what I call "hit the button" emails, videos and blogging. Whatever you decide to use, there are a ton of services out there, so don't recreate the wheel, don't think that you need to write your own content. You really don't. No offense, but most people won't read it anyway! Just send something, anything, and it will bring business and referrals.

## Events

This is the absolute best way to give back to your clients and Realtor partners. At least twice a year I run a movie event. I rent out a Movie Theater on the Saturday morning after the Friday release date. I've done mostly G-rated (Disney or Pixar) movies since I want my clients there and not dropping off their teenagers! Recently I chose some PG movies, but that's only because it's STAR WARS! You show a big movie like Star Wars and you will gain so much recognition and appreciation from your clients. At the event, I do a meet and greet in the lobby with my team doing the registration. Fifteen minutes before the show I get on stage and introduce myself and my team and say a few words. I then do a fun giveaway. After the event, we do a follow up email thanking them and professionally asking for business. Referrals from my events pay for themselves many times over.

I recently did an event for a Realtor and her clients. I even invited some of my clients that didn't have a known Realtor. We used a 100-person theater and showed Cars 3. It was a blast and has paid for itself several times over. Just doing events with agents, helping them build or preserve their business, is an activity that builds great loyalty. What a great way to show how much you care and that you want part in the active conversion of clients for their business.

## Continuous Training & Support

Besides being a Star Wars fan, I'm also a news and research junkie, especially when it comes to this industry. I'm often inspired to write articles about current events or issues and share them with my partners and clients. This serves several purposes that benefit everyone by sharing information and insights that can help both my partners and our future clients. These are not provided as cut-and-paste content for partners to use, rather as a way to start conversations, share valuable ideas, and establish credibility and visibility with clients and community.

(As an example, I've added an article I wrote recently called "Rent vs. Own" to the resources section at the end of this book for your review.)

# *Week 6*

# FINAL REVIEW AND WRAP UP!

Now is the time to review all tasks and action plans resulting from each stage and identifying what the Agent (and you) can do for the finishing touches. What you will find 90% of the time is that the Agent isn't even close to fully implementing anything. Your job as coach is to spend this time pushing through the remaining items to completion. Here you will also look at all the action plans with a fresh eye. Ask yourself: Is this required? Does this fall into their Top 3 or ONE thing? Does it align with helping to accelerate and achieve their defining purpose?

If Agents seem overwhelmed, take the time to review with them and define what and where their focus should be. I often find that when you deviate from your defining statement and get distracted from your core initiatives, that's when overwhelm creeps in and discouragement takes over.

For instance, I was working with a couple recently who were frustrated at the end of each day, feeling like they were making little to no progress.

When I talked to them, we focused on the definition of their perfect day. It went a little something like this: "Initial client sessions, go see homes, negotiate contacts, go to settlements, and go home." Looking back at their daily routines, they could see that they had strayed from that initial path. They were doing things that weren't on their list, and neglecting others that should have been priorities. Bottom line, your life and work day will be a whole lot less stressful (and more productive) if you stick to your guns when it comes to what helps you achieve your perfect day. Define it, and focus on those things. Everything else should be delegated!

The last week is all about reviewing where you started to where you are now and the direction that should be clear in the mind of the Agent. At a minimum, the Agent has a road map and over the next year you can help implement it. Honestly, I've found that the more you can "do" for the Agent during your time together, the more they will thank and value you. As for myself, if all else fails, I attempt to impress upon them at least one of my core initiatives to help their business. I keep harping on this thing called Home Scout. Whether you use the service or not, what you are looking for is a quick an easy implementation of your tools to help the agent. The idea behind the initiatives I use with my agents is that it encourages focus, provides clear goals, gives predictive analysis, and allows a Realtor to do something they have never, ever done before—forecast revenue.

# Chapter 10

## EVALUATION OF THE
# RELATIONSHIP

———————

After you've completed the 6 weeks of coaching work, there is a very important last step: Schedule a call/meeting each quarter with re-evaluation at the one year mark.

Out of sight = out of mind, right? That's why it's so important to stay in touch. It's quite easy to make a phone call or schedule a lunch or coffee once each quarter. And the results for your time can be tremendous. Be sure to allot your time wisely. For instance, I'm not taking an Agent to a nice lunch that I don't like and who doesn't do any business with me. Remember, pour your efforts on partners that you enjoy working with and add leverage to your business.

*Special Note: I don't want the reader to get the impression that the agents that I haven't followed up with are agents I don't like. Sometimes it's a "good intentions by the wayside" sort of thing. It happens to all of us. Forgive yourself and do your best to reconnect and stay connected.*

You'd think I have some grand grading system of who I take out to lunch and who I don't. I don't do that. I simply look at who I want to work with, and who I think has potential to do more with me as a partner. I've had high producing Agents that literally don't want to meet with me. They just don't have time. They don't want coaching, they don't want lunch... they just don't care for any of that. Yet they send me business! They receive quarterly communications from me based on their "preferred method of contact" and that's enough contact for them! P.s. Although I feel phone is the best form of communication outside of a meeting, email has its benefits. Even texting! Just remember to communicate in the manner that the Agent prefers. It's simple.

There should always be a review at the one-year mark. Before you contact them, ask yourself (and your team) what the current level of engagement is, and if you want more. Could be that you may not work well together or you may have to make a personnel switch on your team. Maybe the leads started out great but have dropped off. Or maybe the Agent is stuck in a rut and needs your help. Whatever it is, get some ammunition before you contact. When you call, or meet, the first question should be "How do you like working with my team?" Followed by, "What do you feel we could do better to help your business and your clients?"

Again, always look for the "thank you." I constantly ask what more we can do to help their clients. I'm seeking to identify what value needs to be added or continue to be added for us to be their top lender. This is pretty much how I phrase the question or even make the statement. I tell the Agent that my team and I want to be their #1 Loan Officer choice for all clients. If we aren't there or risk losing our spot, I want to know what value can I bring to get us (or keep us) there. These are valid questions and they should be spoken with sincerity and humility. You are there to help their business and not just stand there with your hand out.

Review "the problem" and ask if your professional relationship helped solve it. Perhaps the Agent will realize that they haven't changed so you didn't even have a chance to help! Perhaps they are stuck in their ways and still losing 90% of the people they speak to. Or maybe you are seeing only 5 to 10% of their contacts too late in the process. Impress upon them that you are there to solve the problem in their business and that getting you involved up front and early in the buyer education phase is paramount to their success. Let them know in no uncertain terms that you aren't afraid to put in the extra work to make more clients and more sales happen for them!

If you feel that you have the right foundation for working together, then reset the one year plan. Investigate if coaching is something they will need. See if they need to implement one of your initiatives. Perhaps you'll invest money together in an event. Whatever it is, this is the point where you decide to pursue or cut the cord.

Cutting the cord doesn't have to be a dramatic incident, though. In fact, I don't ever "cut off" an agent unless it's a very unsavory situation. I'm the King of onesie-twosie Agents. Meaning I may get 1 to 2 deals a year with them, and the only thing I'm doing for them is keeping them on my email campaigns and perhaps my $5/month business boost. $60 a year is worth one deal, and I say keep them coming!

# Chapter 11

## FINAL
### WORDS

---

I hope you can see the method to my madness when adding value to (and choosing) a Realtor partner. If you have any questions as to the specifics of anything written herein, please don't hesitate to reach out to me at **loans@elmendorfteam.com**—this is our personal email. One of the things I enjoy most is helping other Loan Officers succeed. And quite frankly, every time I coach or have a one hour quick-coach call with a Loan Officer, I learn something.

# Chapter 12

## MY
## STORY

---

Everyone remembers many important and impactful days in their lives, ones they will never forget. Days of joy, love, hurt or sadness...days of victory and defeat.

Of the many days I remember, my marriage to my wonderful wife of 22 years, the birth of my 2 children, and my 4 holes-in-one (yes I remember them all...along with the 2 leaners!). But most of all, the most memorable day was on a warm Wednesday night, 23 years ago.

It was the first Wednesday night service I'd ever attended at Fairfax Baptist Temple. I don't remember the message but Bud Calvert always had a way of getting the message of salvation through each time. I'm sure it was a culmination of his messages over the past month I'd been attending and the Holy Spirit putting in some overtime. That night I finally surrendered.

I bowed my head in the dimly lit parking lot of Fairfax Baptist Temple and asked God to save me. I remember pleading with God to save me. That I wasn't sure of my salvation and I accepted Jesus into my heart and His payment on the cross for me. Jesus Christ shed His precious blood and paid the cost for my sin. He took my place of punishment and sorrow and rose again the 3rd day victorious. I believed that and in that moment, I was saved. Saved from eternal damnation and the wrath of God. Heaven is my new home.

My brother was the first to share God's plan of salvation with me. Trey Elmendorf, my dear brother who went home to be with the Lord just over a year ago. I will never know the countless hours he prayed for me and, more than that, actively sought to share the gospel with me. I remember clearly one night we had a phone call. I was lying on my brother's bed in the basement of our old home, 18 years old and recently dumped by my girlfriend. I was still dealing with the loss of our mother earlier that year as well. Trey told me of a friend who would never leave or forsake me. I love you, Trey, and will see you soon.

I feel that it was only fitting to finish this book with my personal story and how you can also have peace with God, true fellowship, and know for sure that Heaven is your home. I hope you will indulge the following thoughts I have for you concerning your eternal destination.

1 John 1:3 says, "That which we have seen and heard declare we unto you, that ye also may have fellowship with us: and truly our fellowship is with the Father, and with his Son Jesus Christ."

## True fellowship with God comes:

1.  When you recognize that your sin has separated you from a Holy God.
2.  When you acknowledge that just punishment for your sin is death in Hell.
3.  When you realize that your salvation cannot be earned by being a good person, but rather it is a gift from God.
4.  When you accept that God paid the price for your sin when Jesus Christ died in your place on the cross.
5.  When you ask God to save you by calling on the name of Jesus Christ.

When one repents of their sin and accepts Jesus Christ as their personal Lord and Savior, they are saved. The Bible tells us that saved people are free from the penalty of sin and will avoid the judgment of God to come. We will be in Heaven for all eternity with our God. It is then our responsibility to declare the free gift that God has so graciously offered to all who will believe.

**The Next Step:** Ask God to save you by praying the sinner's prayer.

## What is the sinner's prayer?

The sinner's prayer is offered to God when someone realizes that they are a sinner and in need of a Savior. Saying a sinner's prayer will not accomplish anything on its own. A true sinner's prayer only represents what a person knows, understands, and believes about their sinfulness and need for salvation.

The first aspect of a sinner's prayer is understanding that we are all sinners. Romans 3:10 proclaims, "As it is written, there is none righteous, no, not one." The Bible makes it clear that we have all sinned. We are all sinners in need of mercy and forgiveness from God (Titus 3:5-7). Because of our sin, we deserve eternal punishment (Matthew 25:46). The sinner's prayer is a plea for grace instead of judgment. It is a request for mercy instead of wrath.

The second aspect of a sinner's prayer is knowing what God has done to remedy our lost and sinful condition. God took on flesh and became a human being in the Person of Jesus Christ (John 1:1,14). Jesus taught us the truth about God and lived a perfectly righteous and sinless life (John 8:46; 2 Corinthians 5:21). Jesus then died on the cross in our place, taking the punishment that we deserve (Romans 5:8). Jesus rose from the dead to prove His victory over sin, death, and hell (Colossians 2:15; 1 Corinthians chapter 15). Because of all of this, we can have our sins forgiven and be promised an eternal home in Heaven - if we will just place our faith in Jesus Christ. All we must do is believe that He died in our place and rose from the dead (Romans 10:9-10). We can be saved by grace alone, through faith alone, in Jesus Christ alone. Ephesians 2:8 declares, "For it is by grace you have been saved, through faith - and this not from yourselves, it is the gift of God."

Saying the sinner's prayer is simply a way of declaring to God that you are relying on Jesus Christ as your Savior. There are no "magical" words that result in salvation. It is only faith in Jesus' death and resurrection that can save us. If you understand that you are a sinner and in need of salvation through Jesus Christ, here is a sinner's prayer you can pray to God.

"God, I know that I am a sinner.
I know that I deserve the consequences of my sin.
However, I am trusting in Jesus Christ as my Savior.
I believe that His death and resurrection
provided for my forgiveness.
I trust in Jesus and Jesus alone as
my personal Lord and Savior.
Thank you, Lord, for saving me and forgiving me!
Amen!"

Did you pray the sinner's prayer and truly understand and believe what it teaches? If so, please email me at **rick@elmendorfteam. com** and let me know. Secondly, you should get involved in a local, bible-believing church. To find a church in your area, you can use this website: **http://bn66.com/churches/baptist.html**. When you arrive, let the pastor know of your decision to accept Christ as your Savior.

I pray for each of you reading this book that it will not only affect your business but also your life.

In His Service,

Rick Elmendorf

# ABOUT THE AUTHOR

Recently recognized as one of the Top 1% Mortgage Originators in America, Rick Elmendorf is known for helping real estate agents thrive by applying structured systems supporting the right relationships for igniting growth and creating a businessand life— they always dreamed of.

With 25 years of experience and growth rates that consistently place him among the most successful loan officers in the nation, Rick has built his business on a systematic approach to building strong relationships with the right people who will add value and uplift each other's business.

The existing relationships between loan officers and Realtors, quite frankly, is broken. In his book, "The Loan Officer Revolution," Rick offers his solution—and a detailed system—for fixing how loan officers, Realtors, and industry professionals create and add value to partnerships that will accelerate business growth for long-term results.

You CAN have a life and have an exceptionally successful business, it's all about connecting with the right people and having the right system in place. A system that this book lays out, step-by-step, for creating partnerships with Realtors that will put life back into your business, instead of sucking the joy out of it.

In 2016, Rick's business volume increased over 30%, with his best year ever at near $210 million with 560 units. His experience and expertise has made him a sought-after industry speaker and he has presented from the stage at top industry events in Atlantic City, Washington D.C., and Las Vegas over the last few years. As a mentor and coach, Rick's ultimate goal is to not only provide the highest quality training, but also to help his colleagues create a life and business rich with joy and success.

Rick resides in the metro DC area, with his wife and business partner of 22 years, and their two sons. Learn more and connect with Rick at **www.rickelmendorf.com**.

# RESOURCES

The Power of Good Partnerships (online presentation):
**http://presentation.loanwithrick.com**

E-Mortgage Analyzer Website: **http://ema.loanwithrick.com**

NexGen HBM: **https://www.nexgenhbm.com/**

Caliber Home Loans: **www.caliberhomeloans.com**

Ultimate Homebuying Experience:
**www.ultimate.loanwithrick.com**

Happy Grasshopper: **www.HappyGrasshopper.com**

MBS Highway: **www.MBShighway.com**

Leadership 360 program: **http://www.performance-experts.com/programs/leadership_360.asp**

## Rick Elmendorf
**rick@elmendorfteam.com**

4050 Legato Road, Suite 100
Fairfax, VA 22033 USA
(571) 249-5363

# RENT VS. OWN

*(a partner & client resource)*

## To rent, or not to rent...that is the question!

This debate is be-coming more and more popular as many people sit on the fence of home-ownership as they wonder whether renting or owning is the right thing to do financially. In fact, even though many people would love to own, unfortunately they've been misinformed as to their ability to do so. The good news is that I'm not here to try to get you to buy a home. On the contrary, I want to share some cold hard facts and the math behind the age-old question of "should I rent, or should I buy" in order to help you make an informed decision.

**What are the barriers to owning a home?** The barriers to home ownership fall within two main issues (a bit like a duel-edged sword): credit and personal decision.

**Mythbusting the Monthly Payment.** Right out of the box, I'd like to tackle that the "monthly payment" is not actually a barrier to buying. Even though that is one of the most important factors to consider, it's fits in more as part of the decision of whether or not to rent or own. We'll get into that later.

## Credit

If your credit is below 620 then you are in a bit of a pickle if you want to own a home. Most lenders set 620 as the drop dead mark of what they will even consider. Some lenders will accept as low at 580 but there have to be some serious compensating factors. Bottom line, credit is a big deal and if your score is 620 or less, then time (and perhaps some credit repair) is your best solution.

**Down Payment.** What about down payment? Isn't this a barrier to owning? Quick answer...not really. The only time this actually becomes a barrier is for high income earners who don't qualify for down payment assistance and don't have the necessary minimum down payment. We'll also discuss down payment solutions later.

**Debt to Income ratios.** Fancy way to say that you don't qualify for home ownership. If you decide to rent, it's not as much of an issue.

## Your personal decision

This may sound weird, but I've met people who just want to keep their options open and don't want to own! They don't want to bog themselves down in one place and feel stuck. Maybe they aren't sure if they will like the place or be happy long term in this home or neighborhood. Maybe they look at owning as a risk and feel that renting provides more security. Either way you cut it, sometimes the decision to rent isn't backed by logic or math, it's just personal preference...and that's OK.

**Is Renting or Owning the right decision?** Now let's make the assumption that you want to own at some point in the future and there aren't any foreseeable barriers in doing so. We are just looking to decide if it's the right decision.

What do we need to consider?

## Monthly Payment

This is the biggie in the mind of most potential home buyers. "Will I pay more if I buy than if I rent?" Good question. The answer is that we have to look at a few more items than just rent payment vs mortgage payment. First, we need to compare the total amount of rent payments to the total amount of mortgage payments for the time you would own. We also have to factor in that rent payments increase at least every 1-2 years (unless you have an amazing landlord!). Mortgage payments are fixed. Add it all up and you'll have your total cash outlay. It's been my experience that when you factor in rent payments over a 5-6 year period that owning comes out even or a tad ahead.

It is possible that renting can be cheaper for the short term. Typically I see this happen when the client rents a smaller home or a home in a less desirable location. This may be an OK decision to get the payments down especially if it's going to be temporary.

## Down payment

If you don't have the funds for a down payment to buy a home this is definitely something to consider! In fact, it may be a barrier to buying, but keep reading...there is help!

- **Down Payment Assistance Programs (DPA).** Across our country there exist many, many down payment assistant programs that can sometimes provide up to the entire down payment for the purchase of a new home. Some are low or interest-free loans that only get paid back when you sell. Others are grants from government entities designed to help people achieve the dream of home ownership. Obviously look for the grants first, then the down payment loans. These types of assistance programs have income restrictions.

- **Low Down Payment Programs.** If you don't qualify for DPA programs, consider a low money down program. There are conventional programs now with as little as 3% down payment and government programs requiring only 3.5% with pretty much any credit score considered! Considering that renting typically requires 1st and last month's rent and a security deposit, you are looking at minimum of 3 to a max of 5 rent payments! Just 3 rent payments can equal about 2% of the purchase price... so you're closer than you think!

- **Gift Funds.** If you can't do DPA and don't have money in the bank, consider getting a gift. Gift are allowed to pay the down payment for the purchase of a new home. Considering you qualify for a 3% to 3.5% down payment program, the amount of the gift may not need to be egregious. Zillow did a really nice write up on the rules of using gift funds when getting a mortgage.

- **Retirement Funds.** Last and definitely least in my books is the use of retirement funds for a down payment. I normally shy away from suggesting this as I feel your money should be working and not being used until retirement, but I do appreciate the fact that there may exist a circumstance where the use of these funds is important to get the home you need. The good thing about retirement funds is that when you pay them back, you are paying back YOU! That's right, you are essentially borrowing from yourself so you pay yourself back the interest. Additionally lenders won't count this payment against your debt-to-income.

## Return on Investment (ROI)

No one will probably tell you this, but your down payment directly affects the rate of return on your new investment. So when you rent, you have no return on investment. There is no ownership, therefore no investment. When you own, you used the down payment (that's your initial investment). And when you sell, you will have cash on hand, that's your return. Now consider you put down 3% on a $400,000 home. That's a $12,000 initial investment. At the end of 5 years, you walk away with $73,000. That's a 608% ROI, or more than 50% per year. This may seem to be a ridiculous example, but it's actually not. Real life numbers of a recent purchase. Imagine now that you bought that same home using a down payment grant, i.e. you put ZERO money down. I really don't need to do the math for you. Case in point, the more money you put down on a home, the lower your ROI! Money does not grow sitting in the equity of your home and it certainly doesn't grow sitting in the bank of your landlord!

**How long will you be in the home?** The shorter the time you will be in the home, the higher the risk for buying. I've found a comfortable time to be over 3 years. If you have at minimum 3 years in the home you will have more benefits than negatives. As mentioned above, sometimes renting for the short term can be cheaper. If you know you're moving (or potentially moving... it's up in the air) then unless you are getting a smoking deal on a new home, just rent. Renting, although more expensive over the long term, leaves your options open which is a good thing. Warning: Don't use that statement as a scapegoat! And don't be afraid of committing to a owning a new home just to "leave your options open." Commitment issues like that could really hurt your financial future. (see more about "dangers" below!)

## Cost to sell

The most recent study shows the average buyer is expected to stay in their home 13 years! However, if you are like me and have moved several times during the past 10 years, you need to consider the cost to selling your home. The cost to sell include Realtor commissions (buyer and listing Agent) and any closing costs paid on behalf of the buyer. There are minimal settlement charges as well. Typically these add up to 6-8% on the high end. I use 6% as the costs to sell since typically the buyer closing costs and others are "built in" to the sales price.

## Appreciation

Home prices normally increase in value. This has been consistent throughout most of history; however, if you weren't under a rock in 2007 you witnessed a devastating time for home prices. It was the largest measure of home depreciation we've seen since the Depression. The financial crisis, the meltdown... it was awful. People who purchased homes in 2005-2006 and after the bubble burst saw a slew of foreclosures, short sales, etc. with the primary reason being the absolute collapse in home values. People were mortgaging their way to financial freedom and then decided to "let go" when home prices crashed. Some foreclosures happened due to a real "life event" but most home owners just "let it go." They bought and bailed adding further to the depreciation slide of home values.

I mention all this to set the stage to the fact that we are now SO regulated (I should know!) that this sort of financial collapse has very little chance of happening again. I've been saying for years that we wouldn't see bank lending rates very high due to the regulation of the banking industry in 1987 and that's held firm. Since the financial reform of 2008 every facet of the dollar sign as it relates to the consumer is highly regulated.

So home prices are going up. Here is a great resource from the National Association of Realtors. Find your market and you will see that home prices are going up. In some parts of the country, you're seeing 5% and up. In my area it's about 4%. On a $400,000 home purchase, 4% means a $16,000 increase in the home value! Factoring appreciation as a buying decision is important. If you own now, that means that your home will expect to grow in value which builds equity. Owning a home has always been considered one of the best investments one can make. However, appreciation can also be a negative factor. We will look at this more in the dangers of not buying.

## Tax Benefits

Home ownership has its benefits. Think of it in its simplest form. The tax benefit of home ownership actually reduces your effective house payment. So let's say you bought that $400,000 home and put 3% down, financing the rest at a rate of 4.125%. The amount of interest you would have paid in the first year is $15,879. The estimated tax benefits would be $4,446. This is the estimated amount you would "get back" from Uncle Sam. So, when I say this reduces your house payment, here's what I mean. With the extra $4,000 you get back in taxes, I recommend a change in how much is withheld from your paycheck. Owning a home will allow you to increase the number of exemptions you take on your W4 which will increase your take home pay! A bigger paycheck just effectively lowered your mortgage payment. This increase in your spendable income can and should be considered when "stretching" for that home of your dreams. When you rent, you have zero tax benefits and will continue to get hammered by the tax man. When you own, the effective payment on a mortgage is lower due to the inherent tax benefits.

## Remaining principal on the loan

Your mortgage payment consists of Principal, Interest, Taxes and Insurance. That "principal" piece is the only good part of your payment! If you look at an amortization schedule for a 30-year loan, you will see that more gets applied to the "principal" portion every month! This simply pays down your loan balance. For the above example on a $400,000 home purchase, borrowing $388,000 at 4.125% interest, at the end of just one year the balance is lower by $6,686. It's sort of a forced saving plan.

## What are the dangers of not owning?

Now that we've discussed the major things to consider, let's discuss the dangers of not owning. In my opinion, before you make the decision not to own, you have to be OK with the following.

- **Higher monthly payments:** If you choose to rent, you could just be paying more, especially when you factor in rising rents vs. a fixed mortgage payment. Figure out the total amount of payments over your expected tenure in the home.

- **Loss of tax benefits:** Over the term of being in the home you would have been able to write off all the interest on the loan. That's like getting 28% of your interest paid back in CASH from Uncle Sam. Take the total amount of interest paid over the term of your time in the home and multiply by 28%. This will be a BIG number.

- **Loss of equity:** Remember that when you pay rent you aren't investing in yourself, but rather paying your landlord's mortgage. Every payment made on a mortgage reduces the amount owed on the loan. So really, whose debt do you want to pay down—yours, or your landlord's? Or rather, who would you rather invest in? You, or your landlord?

# The Cost of Waiting

- **Appreciation:** When a home appreciates, if you are the owner, you earn equity. If you are sitting on the sideline and not the owner, all you can do is watch the home go up in price. Every month... tick, tick, tick. We are expecting a 4.8% increase to home values this year. See the chart below for some math.

- **Interest rates:** When rates go up, payments go up and the cost for the same investment goes up. If you are waiting to buy, it's rolling the dice on interest rates. If rates go up the projected .78% in the next year, this will result in much larger payments.

- **Loss of purchasing power:** This is the real danger! The combination of appreciation and interest rates are the perfect storm. If you wait to buy and both home appreciations and interest rates start climbing, the same home you are looking at today is not only worth more, but will cost more. To keep your payments in line with what you are looking at today, you would have to purchase a cheaper home. The question is, what does that cheaper home look like to you today? Well, that's the home you may have to settle for if you wait until next year or down the road. That, or else higher home prices and higher interest rates will force you to push your budget more than you may be comfortable with.

## Do You Know The Cost of Waiting?
### Interest Rates Won't Be This Low For Long!

If you are one of the many Americans debating purchasing a home but are not sure if you will *buy now* or **wait until next year**, here is a simple example of the impact interest rates & prices will have on your monthly mortgage payment.

| Today | | Next Year |
|---|---|---|
| 4.02% | **Interest Rate** <br> *Freddie Mac Projection 2018* | 4.80% |
| $250,000 | **Home Price** <br> *CoreLogic Projection (+4.9%)* | $262,250 |
| $1,196.42 | **Mortgage Payment** <br> *Per Month - Principal & Interest* | $1,375.93 |

*The Cost of Waiting to Buy is defined as the additional funds it would take to buy a home if prices & interest rates were to increase over a period of time.*

| Increase in Payments: | Monthly | Annually | Over 30 Years |
|---|---|---|---|
| | **$179.51** | **$2,154.12** | **$64,624** |

### Looking for a home that is more expensive than the $250,000 example above?

For *every* $250,000 you borrow, your monthly mortgage payment will increase by $179.51 & the home price will increase by $12,250!

**Here is an example:**
*Mortgage payment is principal & interest only & accounts for a mortgage for the full home price.*

| | Today | Next Year | Cost of Waiting |
|---|---|---|---|
| | 4.02% | 4.80% | |
| | $750,000 | $786,750 | +$36,750 |
| | $3,589.27 | $4,127.80 | +$538.53 |

Sources: CoreLogic, Freddie Mac, Bankrate

# Conclusion

The last thing I want to do is make a blanket statement that it's better to own than to rent. I don't feel that's always the case and it's important to analyze the specific situation of each potential home owner to make the right decision. I hope this shed some light on the positives and negatives of owning vs. renting to help you make an informed decision.

Want more? Don't hesitate to reach out to me at: **loans@elmendorfteam.com**.

# The Problem:
## LOST CONTACTS / BUYERS

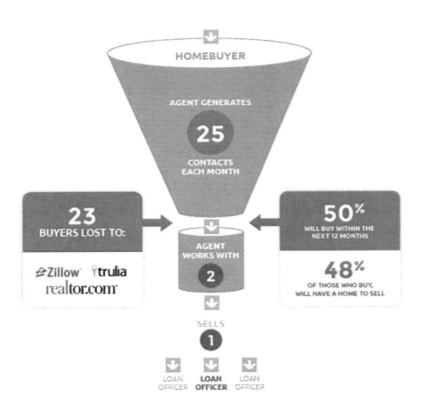

_the problem:_
**LOST CONTACTS/BUYERS**

# A DESCRIPTIVE ACCOUNT OF THE
## *Sales Process*

This is Tom and Judy Smith and this is our personal account of our home-buying experience. My wife and I met with our real estate agent James 4 months ago on the dot to start our journey of home ownership. We are first-time home buyers and were very excited, yet nervous about our upcoming home purchase. We know James, our Realtor, from church and felt comfortable with him. We trust him. That first night James went through the process and how he would help us find our dream home. He gave us some other neat tools as well to aide in finding the perfect home. That night, however, it was mentioned to us that it was time to start thinking about how we would finance our new home.

Financing, great. What a hassle! That's all we could remember from the stories that Sam and Jenny told us about the nightmare of getting a mortgage and going through the very painful process of becoming a homeowner. We really hoped that the mortgage guy James was referring to us would make things easy. There was no way we would use that "other guy" Sam and Jenny put up with last year.

The next morning as I was checking my email, I saw it. 10:32 p.m., an email from James. It was a very nice introduction to Rick Elmendorf, his mortgage guy. All of Rick's contact information was there and he was cc'd on the email. James mentioned in the email that Rick was a true professional, very trustworthy and really knows his stuff. He mentioned that Rick has a team helping him with his clients to make sure nothing is missed during the process.

"Everything will happen on time with no surprises. I trust Rick and his team to make this an enjoyable experience!" was the exact quote. Feeling a little better now...

James continued and said that Rick or someone from his team would be contacting us sometime tomorrow but that if we wanted to get a head start on things to simply go to his website and start the process there. Rick is notified immediately upon receipt of a new application and would be watching out for ours.

So I couldn't wait. I clicked on the link and went to the website. There he was! He doesn't look like a battered used car salesman. Ok, where is that Apply Online link? There it is. Ok, so the whole application was pretty easy. Took me 14 minutes, and that's only because I got a call half way through it.

Soon after I clicked submit on the web form I got an email from Rick's office, letting me know that Rick had received our application and would be in touch shortly.

Rick called later that day and we talked for about 15 minutes on the phone. He went over our loan application and answered some questions I had about financing in general. He said the next steps were that he would get with his team and work up a detailed estimate and attach our approval letter in an email within the next 24 hours. Rick asked if we needed something sooner and he would do it. We weren't in a huge rush, but were looking very much forward to the numbers. He mentioned that his team would be assisting him throughout the process so to expect correspondence from people besides just him.

The next morning we got a phone call from Marie calling from Rick Elmendorf's office. She was checking to see if we got the email with the numbers and the approval letter. I jumped on my email and there it was! Boy these guys are on top of things. Marie asked if now was a good time to discuss, and I said sure. We spent about 15 minutes on the phone going over the estimate. She explained how to manipulate the spreadsheet to show different numbers and how to change the approval letter. She referenced a tab on the spreadsheet that had a list of all the "stuff" I would need to put together to get a loan. I noticed Rick and my agent James were copied on the email. After we were done, she mentioned, "Rick is in the office, would you like to speak to him about anything?" I said sure, I was curious about how this whole team thing would work. I was put on hold and 20 seconds later, Rick picked up and I could hear the smile on his face. "Hey it's Rick! How is everything?"

I said things were just fine and that I was curious as to whom Judy and I would be working with. Rick explained that he had Marie and other team members that would be assisting him on our home purchase and that any of us would be available throughout the process. He mentioned that once you go under contract; he would have a specific Processor assisting Marie and himself to get the loan to closing. Rick went on to say that he is big on making sure that our loan was properly managed throughout the process and that our home purchase closed on time and there were no unwelcome surprises. Rick said that he oversaw everything. I understood that he obviously can't do everything and that is why he has very capable people, "the best in the business" as he put it, assisting him. He re-iterated the importance of having all our financial information to him early on to mitigate any potential issues and be ready to move when things happen.

So it was house-hunting time. I put together my laundry list and uploaded everything to Rick's private web portal. Side note: I remembered one of the big issues that our friends had when getting a mortgage was that they were continually asked for the same things over and over and that the only way they could send their loan officer things was via email (unsecure!) or by fax. I already see just how much more efficient this is! Ok...I digress, but after uploading everything I got an email from the team confirming that they got the documents. How novel!

I also remember that during my first chat with Marie, she had mentioned a great tool called the Home Buyer's Scouting report which Judy and I used ad-nauseam. Our journey searching for the perfect home continued for about 8 weeks. During that time we heard from Rick in an email alert every other week. It was a pretty neat video message which explained what was happening in the market and some good info for those still out there looking. Rick always gave a good insight on trends and rates, everything that would affect us as homebuyers.

Finally our search ended. We found it. The perfect home was this rambler in Alexandria. It was blocks from our favorite restaurant and not too far from my job downtown. I emailed Rick that we wanted to take a look at financing options on the home. I got an email back from Marie in about 30 minutes with an updated estimate. The phone rang. It was Marie, "Hi, this is Marie from Rick's office. How are you?! I was just checking to see that you got the numbers that Rick worked up?" I was very thankful and asked a million questions. It was becoming real now. I got Judy on the phone as she had some further questions about the process. About 15 minutes later, all my questions were answered – for now, I thought. Marie mentioned, "Rick is in the office, would you like to speak with him?" We answered, "No... no need to bother him, you answered all our questions. Wish us luck on the offer!"

We presented our offer and after 2 counter offers and another email back and forth with The Elmendorf Team, we got word from our agent that our offer was accepted! I heard from James that Rick actually helped us seal the deal with his "Offer Accepted" program where he makes a proactive call to the listing agent, makes a guarantee, and I guess just does his thing! Whatever it was it worked, closing would take place at the end of the month. Oh my, that's 28 days from now. We called Rick's office and let Marie, who answered the phone, know we got the home and asked her what we needed to do now. Rick got on the phone with us and said that he would be reserving our interest rate and would officially get things rolling today. He said the next steps were that one of his other assistants would be taking the reins to assist him in setting the loan up for the processor. It was all mumbo-jumbo to me, but I understood that there were certain people now involved that would handle this through closing.

About 10 minutes after our call, we got an email. Rick and our agent James were copied. It was an official looking "Getting Things Rolling" email with an introduction to how the rest of the process would go. There would be a welcome call from someone on Rick's team and they would be updating me at 4 key points during the process. The first was at loan approval, the second when the appraisal came back, then 7 days prior to loan closing, and lastly before closing to review the actual settlement statement. I felt so at ease that nothing would fall through the cracks. I was in good hands.

Later that day I got a call from Michelle. I was at lunch, but called her right back. "Thank you for calling The Elmendorf Team, this is Michelle, how may I help you?" I introduced myself and she thanked me for calling back. Michelle started off by saying how thankful she was to be working with me and my wife and that everyone on the Elmendorf Team was honored to be helping us with our new home purchase. She said her role was simply to make sure that we closed on time with no surprises and that she would be the one monitoring the entire process for Rick. We spent a few minutes over the phone updating some of the application information and she asked me to fax a bank statement and pay stub. She said that she would be submitting our file to processing later today. She confirmed our loan amount, our proposed payments, and that our rate was locked. "Do you have any other questions for me?" We said nope. "Rick is in the office, would you like to speak with him?" I said, "Yes actually, I do need to tell him something."

In just a moment, Rick was on the phone. "Hi Tom, how are things! What can I do for you?" I explained to Rick how impressed I was thus far and remembered that Frank from my office was thinking about buying a home with his wife. I asked if I could give Rick's name to my friend. Rick asked if I instead make an introduction to his friend via email and to copy him. Then, he and his team would take it from there. I thanked him again. Boy, this was really not the nightmare I heard it would be.

Within the next couple of days I got a call from a very pleasant lady name Kelly. She said that she was the processor with Rick's team and would be the handling all the paperwork from here on out. She said that our loan was conditionally approved and only had a couple questions and one or two things to get. She told me that she was the best point of contact from here on out and to call her with any questions or concerns.

The next time we heard from anyone was about a week later. Michelle phoned us to let us know that our appraisal was back and everything was going great. It was "another check off the list and one step closer to being the owners of our new home." Michelle told us that Rick was out of the office at this time, but that she would inform him that the appraisal came back with no issues. She emailed us a copy and I saw that she copied our agent as well.

Closing was getting much closer. Our closing was next Monday and I had spoken to Kelly a few times over the last several days and everything was pretty much in order. The phone rang, it was Michelle. "You are one week from closing and I wanted to confirm everything with you. Do you have a moment?" Of course I did! Michelle wanted to go over a document called the closing disclosure. Basically she confirmed the rate, our loan amount, cash to close...and I stopped her and had a couple of questions. In all the commotion and excitement I had forgotten that we had chosen to "buy down" our interest rate and bring more to closing than just the down payment. One less question at closing I'm sure! Michelle was very pleasant and asked if we had any further questions and that she would be in touch prior to closing to go over the "actual numbers" with us before we closed. We had no further questions. Michelle said "Rick is in the office, would you like to speak to him?" No thanks I said, everything was wonderful.

The day had come; we had the movers lined up. Michelle phoned me at 4 p.m. the night before our closing. She said she had reviewed the actual numbers and compared them with our initial loan estimate and that Rick was spot on with the numbers. She asked me to check our inbox for a copy of the final closing disclosure. There it was, the closing disclosure and Rick's latest closing cost estimate. She said that our actual amount was lower and our cash needed at closing was $214.34 less than we estimated. She made sure we understood every charge on the CD and reminded us to have certified funds and to bring our IDs to closing. She said to "please call if you have any questions whatsoever at closing" and to "have fun!!" I thanked her and prepared for our big day.

The closing went without a hitch. The numbers were perfect and 28 minutes later we were done signing the paperwork. We were handed the keys to our new home. I made a point to mention to our agent just how easy this process was and thanked him again for everything. My wife and I celebrated that night with a certificate given to us at closing. It was a gift certificate to one of our favorite chain restaurants.

The note read:

> *Congratulations on your new home. We appreciate you as clients and look forward to many more years serving you. I look forward to our annual review.*
>
> *~Rick Elmendorf and Team*

That next Friday we got a call from Rick. He asked how things went and thanked us for allowing him to serve us. He said that our agent James was a great source of business for him and asked if we would definitely recommend to James to continue to refer Rick and his team to anyone he knew that was shopping for a mortgage. "Of course...I'll call James today!" He also mentioned that we should receive a survey and if we wouldn't mind responding to it. "No problem, Rick."

In our inbox was the survey. It was sent by Michelle after our closing date and Rick had been copied which obviously prompted his call.

It said:

> *CONGRATULATIONS on your successful loan closing! I know I speak for the whole team when I say it was a true pleasure to work with you. We need more clients like you! :)*
>
> *It is extremely important to me to know how we performed for you. I am always looking for ways to improve our service and make the loan experience better as well. One of the ways we measure success is by your willingness to refer your co-workers, friends and family to me for a loan or advice.*
>
> *Would you mind answering some quick questions for me? Thanks and we appreciate you giving me the opportunity to serve you.*
>
> **Questions:**
>
> 1. *What made you decide to use us?*
> 2. *Is there anything we could have done better during the transaction and were there any hiccups you felt we could have avoided?*
> 3. *Was there anything we did especially well throughout the process?*
> 4. *What was your overall impression of The Elmendorf Team and would you recommend us to others?*
>
> *Thank you again for choosing The Elmendorf Team to help you finance your new home! We look forward to serving you for many years to come.*

He said that we were such great clients and would appreciate to work with more people like us. I promised to have the survey back to him tomorrow. I completed the survey and wrote a separate thank you note to Rick and his team after closing.

It read:

> *We can't thank you enough for all your help with the home loan. We always heard that getting a mortgage was a stressful event and we weren't looking forward to it. We were so pleased with your service, attention to detail and professionalism. You were always quick and responsive. We felt special. We felt like you truly cared about us. Personally, I really appreciated the fact that Rick was always available for me. I know he was busy, but I felt he always had time for me. This was evident by the team always asking me if I wanted to talk to him. That was truly impressive. The entire team was spectacular. I would without a doubt not only do my next loan with your team, but tell everyone I know that you are the most outstanding set of mortgage professionals in the world. Thank you, thank you, and thank you for making this such a wonderful experience. I pray many blessings for you and your team, Tom and Judy Smith.*

# *Debrief*
## ON DESCRIPTIVE ACCOUNT

- **How to be referred.** 10:32 p.m., an email from James. It was a very nice introduction to Rick Elmendorf, his mortgage guy. All of Rick's contact information was there and he was cc'd on the email. James mentioned in the email that Rick was a true professional, very trustworthy and really knows his stuff. He mentioned that Rick has a team helping him with his clients to make sure nothing is missed during the process. "Everything will happen on time with no surprises. I trust Rick and his team to make this an enjoyable experience!" was the exact quote.

- **Clients will use the website.** So I couldn't wait. I clicked on the link and went to the website.

- **Email confirmation from team after receiving new application.** Soon after I clicked submit on the web form I got an email from Rick's office, letting me know that Rick had received our application and we would be in touch shortly.

- **Initial contact from Loan Officer Assistant or Rick.** Rick called later that day and we talked for about 15 minutes on the phone. He went over our loan paperwork and answered some questions I had about financing in general. He said the next steps were that he would get with the team and work up a detailed estimate and attach our approval letter in an email within the next 24 hours.

- **Immediate follow up call from Account or Opportunity Owner after presentation is sent.** The next morning we got a phone call from Marie calling from Rick Elmendorf's office.

She was checking to see if we got the email with the numbers and the approval letter. Marie asked if now was a good time to discuss, and I said sure.

> **Keep it short.** We spent about 15 minutes on the phone going over the estimate.

> **Explain the EMA.** She explained how to manipulate the spreadsheet to show different numbers and how to change the approval letter.

> **Encourage getting us docs.** She referenced the tab that had all the "stuff" I would need to put together.

> **Relay to the client that Rick and their agent are always in the loop.** I noticed Rick and my agent James were copied on the email.

- **Rick or Opportunity Owner is always available.** After we were done, she mentioned, "Rick is in the office, would you like to speak to him about anything?" I said sure...I was curious about how this whole team thing would work.

> **Owner or Rick answer questions on the spot.** Rick explained that he had Marie and other team members that would be assisting him on our home purchase and that any of us would be available throughout the process. He mentioned that once you go under contract; he had a specific Processor and Production Assistant that get the nod and would be assisting him to get the loan to closing. Rick went on to say that he is big on making sure that our loan was properly managed throughout the process and that our home purchase closed on time and there were no unwelcome surprises.

> **Re-iterate that Owner and Rick are always in the**

**loop and that we have a great team.** Rick said that he oversaw everything. I understood that he obviously can't do everything and that is why he has very capable people, "the best in the business" as he put it, assisting him. He re-iterated the importance of having all our financial information to him early on to mitigate any potential issues and be ready to move when things happen.

- **Always confirm docs received.** I put together my laundry list and uploaded everything. I got an email from the team confirming that they received everything.

- **Get all buyers on the Home Scout and talk about Sold Home Alert.** During my first chat with Marie, she had mentioned a great tool called the Home Buyer's Scouting report which Judy and I used ad-nauseam. *(\*Note that Home Scouting changed to Home Scout effective 2017)*

- **Rick to send personal messages to Pre-Approved buyers every other Friday.** During that time we heard from Rick in an email alert every other week. It was a pretty neat video message which explained what was happening in the market and some good info for those still out there looking.

- **Get in the habit of offering to speak to Rick or Owner.** Marie asked, "Rick is in the office, would you like to speak with him?" We said, "No... no need to bother him, you answered all our questions. Wish us luck on the offer!"

- **Be consistent on how we answer the phone.** Later that day I got a call from Michelle. I was at lunch, but called her right back. "Thank you for calling The Elmendorf Team, this is Michelle, how may I help you?"

- **During every communication THANK the client for working with us.** Michelle started off by saying how thankful she was to be working with me and my wife and that everyone on The Elmendorf Team was honored to be helping us with our new home purchase.

- **Offering speaking to Rick or Owner opens up possibilities for referrals!** "Rick is in the office, would you like to speak with him?" I said, "Yes actually...I do need to tell him something."

  > **Encourage client referrals!** I explained to Rick how impressed I was thus far and remembered that Frank from my office was thinking about buying a home with his wife. I asked if I could give Rick's name to my friend.

  > **Have the client introduce you via email.** Rick asked if I instead make an introduction to his friend via email and that to copy him. Then, he and his team would take it from there.

- **Quick calls from the Processor.** Within a couple of days I got a call from a very pleasant lady name Kelly. She said that she was the processor with Rick's team and would be the handling all the paperwork from here on out.

- **Processor takes ownership.** She told me that she was the best point of contact from here on out and to call her with any questions or concerns.

- **Appraisal Notify.** The next time we heard from anyone was about a week later. Michelle phoned us to let us know that our appraisal was back and everything was going great.

- **7 Day Prior.** The phone rang, it was Michelle. "You are one week from closing and I wanted to confirm everything with you. Do you have a moment?" *(\*Note this is now a 10 day review* *as of Jan 2017)*

- **Rick or Owner are always there!** Michelle said "Rick is in the office, would you like to speak to him?" No thanks I said, everything was wonderful.

- **Closing Disclosure Review (1 day prior).** The day had come; we had the movers lined up. Michelle phoned me at 4 p.m. the night before our closing.

- **Encourage the client to tell their agent how awesome we did.** I made a point to mention to our agent just how easy this process was and thanked him again for everything.

- **Closing Gift with a nice note from Rick.** My wife and I celebrated that night with a certificate given to us at closing. It was a gift certificate to one of our favorite chain restaurants.

The note read:

> *Congratulations on your new home. We appreciate you as clients and look forward to many more years serving you. I look forward to our annual review.*
>
> *~Rick Elmendorf and Team*

- **Weekly Post-Closing Phone calls (client and agents).** That next Friday we got a call from Rick. He asked how things went and thanked us for allowing him to serve us. He said he'd just spoken to both agents and that they were very happy for us as well.

- **Ask the client to call their agent and encourage them to use us more.** He said that our agent James was a great source of business for him and asked if we would definitely recommend to James to continue to refer Rick and his team to anyone he knew that was shopping for a mortgage. "Of course...I'll call James today!"

- **Post-Closing Survey.** He mentioned that we should receive a survey and if we wouldn't mind responding to it.

    > **Rick cc'd on the survey sent by Michelle prompting Rick's call.** In our inbox was the survey. It was sent by Michelle after our closing date and Rick had been copied which obviously prompted his call.